The Letting Go

guided journal

Published in the United States by: Hay House, Inc.: www.hayhouse.com®
Published in Australia by: Hay House Australia Pty. Ltd.: www.hayhouse.com.au
Published in the United Kingdom by: Hay House UK, Ltd.: www.hayhouse.co.uk
Published in India by: Hay House Publishers India: www.hayhouse.co.in

Cover design and Interior Design: Julie Davison

Cataloging-in-Publication Data is on file at the Library of Congress.

Tradepaper ISBN: 978-1-4019-6909-7

10 9 8 7 6 5 4 3 2 1
1st edition, November 2022

Printed in the United States of America

The Letting Go

guided journal

How to Remove Your Inner Blocks to Happiness, Love, and Success

DAVID R. HAWKINS, M.D., Ph.D.

HAY HOUSE, INC.
Carlsbad, California • New York City
London • Sydney • New Delhi

Introduction

The Letting Go Guided Journal gives the reader a greater understanding and hands-on experience of what Dr. David R. Hawkins's letting go technique is, and the many benefits it can give in one's life.

The intention is for the reader to realize the value of putting into practice the letting go method and, through the prompts and exercises, know firsthand the liberation one feels after letting go of the long-standing fears, blocks, inhibitions, and suffering that are common to all of us as human beings. To have the direct experience of inner freedom and newfound self-assurance are just a couple of the benefits one can have.

It is suggested to do the exercises in the order presented. Dr. Hawkins wrote his book *Letting Go* in a particular sequence, where one first lets go of the lower, negative emotions and programs, which most likely have been suppressed and repressed in the subconscious. By allowing the energy of the lower emotions to come up, and be processed out, one can truly experience the higher states of consciousness. It is important that you take your time with each exercise, as there is no time limit here, nor is there any need to rush the process. There are also extra pages in the back of the journal if you need more room to write for any of the entries.

Inspirational quotes by Dr. Hawkins are also interspersed in each section, adding deeper meaning to the value of the exercises and the personal outcomes one can realize. Since the prompts and exercises are interactive, a person uses their own personal experiences and interpersonal relationships to apply the letting go method in their everyday life. In this way, one's life becomes their teacher.

Dr. Hawkins's love for mankind shines through in all his lectures and books, and in his devotion to truth. His Map of Consciousness® and the letting go process are at the core of his teaching. He dedicated his life in service to mankind, to the alleviation of human suffering.

With his lighthearted spirit and sense of humor, a person would feel safe, uplifted, and encouraged to continue on their inner journey.

We hope that you feel that same hope, safety, and encouragement as you are working through the pathway of this journal.

The inner journey of yourself is exciting, and the rewards to living a higher, freer, and more enlightened life can be yours.

Congratulations! Your intention to elevate your life by applying the letting go process can only bring you closer to who you truly are.

Are you ready to get started?

— Susan Hawkins
and the Veritas Publishing Staff

The mechanism of surrender
is simple and the truth
is self-evident.

The letting go technique is a pragmatic system of eliminating obstacles and attachments. It can also be called a mechanism of surrender. This approach stands out for its sheer simplicity, efficiency, clinical efficacy, absence of questionable concepts, and rapidity of observable results. Its simplicity is deceptive and almost disguises the real benefit of the technique: to set us free from emotional attachments.

This journal will help you reach great clarity and transcend your problems along the way, not by finding the answers, but by undoing the basis of your problems. The state reached by the great sages of history is available; the solutions are within you and easy to find. There is no dogma or belief system here. You verify everything for yourself, so you cannot be misled. There is no dependence on any teachings. It follows the dicta of "Know thyself," "The truth shall set you free," and "The kingdom of God is within you." It works for the cynic, the pragmatist, the religionist, and the atheist. It works for any age or cultural background. It works for the spiritual person and the nonspiritual person alike.

Because the mechanism is your own, nobody can take it away from you. You are safe from disillusionment. You will find out for yourself what is real and what are just the mind's programs and belief systems. Eventually you will stop listening to your ego, or small self, because you have discovered your greater Self. When you come upon it, you will understand what those great sages were trying to convey. You will understand it because truth is self-evident and within your own Self.

This journal is written with you, the reader, constantly in mind. It is easy, effortless, and enjoyable. There is nothing to learn or memorize. You will become lighter and happier as you use it. The material will automatically start bringing you the experience of freedom as you work through the pages. You are going to feel the inner blocks to your happiness, love, and success being removed. Everything you do will become more enjoyable. You are in for some happy surprises about your life! Things are going to get better and better!

Letting go is like the sudden cessation of an inner pressure or the dropping of a weight. It is accompanied by a sudden feeling of relief and lightness, with an increased happiness and freedom.

Think how great it would be if you could do that all of the time, in any place, and with any event. You could always feel free and happy and never be cornered by your feelings again. That's what this technique is all about: *letting go consciously and frequently at will.* You are then in charge of how you feel, and you are no longer at the mercy of the world and your reactions to it. You are no longer the victim.

The price of holding on to smallness can be demonstrated with muscle testing. The procedure is fairly simple, and you can try it now with a friend: Hold in mind a mean, petty thought and have them press down on your arm while you resist; notice the effect. Now choose the exact opposite view. Picture yourself as being generous, forgiving, loving, and experiencing your inner greatness. Instantly, there will be an enormous increase in muscle strength, indicating a surge of positive bioenergy. Write about what you experienced.

_____

_____

_____

_____

_____

_____

_____

_____

_____

_____

_____

_____

_____

_____

_____

_____

_____

_____

_____

_____

_____

If you are interested in learning more about muscle testing, it is thoroughly covered in the book *Power vs. Force,* as is the Map of Consciousness©. You will find the Map included at the end of this journal so that you can refer to it if you like, but it isn't necessary. All you really need to know is that as you go through the process here, you will be working on letting go of negative feelings and stopping your resistance to the positive emotions. The result will be your inner transformation.

Letting go means simply to let a feeling be there, and then to focus on surrendering the energy behind it. The first step is to allow yourself to have the feeling without resisting it, venting it, fearing it, condemning it, or moralizing about it. It means to drop judgment and to see that it is *just* a feeling. The technique is to be with the feeling and surrender all efforts to modify it in any way. Let go of wanting to resist the feeling. *It is resistance that keeps the feeling going.* When you give up resisting or trying to modify the feeling, it will shift to the next feeling and be accompanied by a lighter sensation. A feeling that is not resisted will disappear as the energy behind it dissipates.

Yet sometimes we surrender a feeling and then notice that it returns or continues. This is because there is more of it yet to be surrendered. We have stuffed these feelings all of our lives and there can be a lot of energy pushed down that needs to come up and be acknowledged. When surrender occurs, there is an immediate lighter, happier feeling, almost like a "high."

By continuously letting go, it is possible to stay in that state of freedom. Feelings come and go, and eventually you realize that you are not your feelings, but that the real "you" is merely witnessing them. You stop identifying with them. The "you" that is observing and is aware of what is happening always stays the same.

The results of letting go are deceptively quick and subtle, but the effects are very powerful. Often we have let go but think that we haven't. It will be our friends who make us aware of the change. One reason for this phenomenon is that, when something is fully surrendered, it disappears from consciousness. Now, because we never think of it, we don't realize that it has gone. This is a common phenomenon among people who are growing in consciousness.

To keep track of progress, it can be helpful to keep a chart of your gains. It is not unusual for people who have made enormous gains to claim, "It just isn't working." We have to remind ourselves sometimes what we were like before we started this process.

So before we go on, write down where you are right now. What are the areas in your life that you think might benefit from the letting go technique? Write in as much detail as possible on the pages that follow.

When letting go, ignore all thoughts.
Focus on the feeling itself.

It is not something new or foreign. It is not an esoteric teaching or somebody else's idea or a belief system. We are merely utilizing our own inner nature to get freer and happier.

When letting go, it's not helpful to "think" about the technique. It's better to just do it. Eventually it will be seen that all thoughts are resistance. They are all images that the mind has made to prevent us from experiencing what actually *is*. When we have been letting go for a while and have begun experiencing what is really going on, we will laugh at our thoughts. Thoughts are fakes, absurd make-beliefs that obscure the truth. Pursuing thoughts can keep us occupied endlessly. We will discover one day that we are right where we started.

Thoughts are like goldfish in a bowl; the real Self is like the water. The real Self is the space between the thoughts or, more exactly, the field of silent awareness underneath all thoughts. Once we have contacted this inner Self, this inner greatness, this inner completion, contentment, and true sense of happiness, we have transcended the world.

We have all had the experience of being so totally absorbed in what we were doing that we scarcely noticed the passage of time. The mind was very quiet, and we were simply doing what we were doing without resistance or effort. We felt happy, maybe humming to ourselves. We functioned without stress. We were very relaxed, although busy. We suddenly realized that we never needed all those thoughts after all.

Recall a time in your life when you felt this way. What were you doing? How did it feel to be in this state? Write about it here.

_____

_____

_____

_____

_____

_____

_____

It is often beneficial to look at some commonly held beliefs and let go of them right in the beginning, such as: (1) We only deserve things through hard work, struggle, sacrifice, and effort; (2) Suffering is beneficial and good for us; (3) We don't get anything for nothing; (4) Things that are very simple aren't worth much. We may also fear that if we let go of a desire for something, we won't get it. Surrendering some of these psychological barriers to the technique itself will allow an enjoyment of its effortlessness and ease.

Make a list of some limiting beliefs you have about success, money, relationships, or health that you would like to use to practice the letting go technique. Journal about your insights, and practice letting go on each one of them.

_____

_____

_____

_____

_____

_____

_____

_____

_____

_____

_____

_____

Letting go of negative feelings is the undoing of the ego, which will be resistant at every turn. This may result in skepticism about the technique, "forgetting" to surrender, a sudden upsurge of escapism, or venting feelings by expressing and acting out. The solution is simply to keep on letting go of the feelings you have about the whole process. Let the resistance be there but don't resist the resistance.

You are free. You don't *have* to let go. Nobody is forcing you. Look at the fear behind the resistance. What are you afraid of regarding this process? Are you willing to let go of that?

_____

_____

_____

_____

_____

_____

_____

_____

_____

_____

_____

_____

_____

It is the nature of the universe that everything in it is represented by its equal and opposite. There is fear, but there is also courage. There is hatred, but its opposite is love. There is timidity, but there is also bravery. The way out of negativity is, therefore, the willingness to acknowledge and let go of negative feelings and, at the same time, the willingness to let go of resisting their positive opposite.

For example, a friend's birthday is coming up and because of things that have happened in the past, we feel unwilling to do anything for them. We are feeling resentful and stingy, and it just seems impossible to get out and shop for a present.

Since the exact opposite feelings of resentment and stinginess are those of forgiveness and generosity, we can choose to imagine the quality of generosity and let go of resisting it. We then see that we actually do enjoy giving to others under certain circumstances. We remember the positive flood of feeling that comes upon us when we express gratitude and acknowledge the gifts that others have given us. We see that we have really been suppressing a desire to forgive and, as we let go of the resistance to being forgiving, there emerges the willingness to let go of the grievance. As we do, we stop identifying with our small self and become consciously aware of our greater Self.

This process is applicable in all negative situations. It enables us to change the context by which we perceive our current situation. It enables us to give it a new and different meaning. It lifts us up from being the helpless victim to the conscious chooser. In the example given, it doesn't mean that we have to rush out and buy a birthday gift. But it does mean that we are now aware that we are in our current position out of choice. We have total freedom, with greater latitude of action and choice. This is a much higher state of consciousness than the helpless victim who is trapped by a past resentment.

Think about a present situation you're having negative feelings about. What are those feelings? When you think of the exact opposite, what are the positive feelings? Now look for those positive feelings within yourself and stop resisting them. As you let go of the resistance to the positive, what was this experience like? What did you notice? Write down what you discovered.

The usual mechanisms that the mind consciously uses to handle emotions are suppression (or repression), expression, and escape. These are deleterious only when they are used without conscious intent. The purpose is to reduce the sheer overwhelming quantity of the emotion itself so that it can be disassembled and let go of in bits and pieces. Thus, in an overwhelm, it is all right *consciously* to push away as much of the emotion as we are capable of at the moment.

The emotion can be reduced in intensity by sharing the feeling with close friends or mentors. By merely expressing the feeling, some of the energy behind it is reduced. It is also all right in this circumstance to consciously utilize escape mechanisms, such as going out in a social situation to get some distance from the upset, playing with the dog, watching television, going to the movies, playing music, making love, or whatever one's habit is under the circumstances. Laughter can also be very helpful, as it assists you in letting go of underlying emotional pressure and canceling negative thoughts.

When the feeling has been reduced in its sheer quantity and intensity, it is best to start letting go of small aspects of the situation rather than the overall situation and the accompanying emotion itself.

To illustrate this point, let's take the example of a man who loses his job after many years with a company, and is now in an overwhelm of despair. By utilizing the three mechanisms already described, some of the emotion can be reduced and he can address some of the smaller things about the job. For instance, could he let go of wanting to have lunch at the place he always went with his colleagues? Could he let go of wanting to park his car in the spot he always had? Could he let go of the attachment to his desk? Could he let go of the attachment to his co-workers and their friendliness toward him? Could he let go of seeing the same boss every day?

The purpose of surrendering these smaller aspects of losing a job, which may seem trivial, is that it gets the mind into the letting go mode. The negative feelings have been acknowledged and worked through; consequently, they've lost their charge. Suddenly there is the awareness that we have the courage to face the situation, recognize our feelings, and do something about them. As the trivia are surrendered, curiously, the main event becomes less and less oppressive.

Try this now. Think of something big in your life you've been struggling to let go of (such as a job, a relationship, or the like). How might you apply the letting go technique to smaller aspects of it, such as in this example? Explore this now.

_____

_____

_____

_____

_____

_____

_____

_____

_____

_____

_____

_____

*You will become more
and more conscious when
you surrender your
negative feelings.*

One of the laws of consciousness is: *We are only subject to a negative thought or belief if we consciously say that it applies to us.* We are free to choose not to buy into a negative belief system.

For negativity to apply to our life, we must first subscribe to it and secondly, give it the energy of belief. If we have the power to make negativity manifest in our life, obviously our mind also has the power to make its converse come true.

How does the law of consciousness that appears on the opposite page work in everyday life? Let's take a common example: The media reports that unemployment is at a record high. The television commentators insist that no jobs are available. At this point, we are free to refuse to buy into the negative thought form. We can say instead, "Unemployment does not apply to me." By refusing to accept the negative belief, it now has no hold over our own life.

How do you feel about this? Can you think of a time in which you found that conventional wisdom about the economy, let's say, didn't actually apply to you? If not, can you foresee how refusing to buy in to a negative belief system might greatly benefit you moving forward? Write your thoughts on this below.

_____

_____

_____

_____

_____

_____

_____

_____

_____

_____

We can simplify the levels of consciousness into three major states: inert, energetic, and peaceful. The first state—inertia—is reflective of the emotional levels of apathy, grief, and fear. They interfere with our concentration on the situation at hand and engage us instead with our own thoughts, most of which are in the realm of "I don't know," "I'm not sure," and "I don't think I can."

Let's begin with apathy. It is the feeling that we cannot do anything about our situation and no one else can help. It is hopelessness and helplessness. It is associated with such thoughts as: "Who cares?"; "What's the use?"; "It's boring."; "Why bother?"; and "I can't win anyway."

Is there a situation in your life right now where you feel hopeless and helpless? Summarize this situation and write down all your thoughts and feelings surrounding it.

_____

_____

_____

_____

_____

_____

_____

_____

_____

_____

_____

Next, make a list of statements that start with "I can't." Then replace the words "I can't" with "I won't." Notice if there is a shift in your energy.

_____

_____

_____

_____

_____

_____

_____

_____

_____

_____

_____

_____

_____

_____

_____

In reality, we are very capable beings, and most "I can'ts" are really "I won'ts." Behind the "I can'ts or the "I won'ts" is frequently a fear. Also, if you find yourself in the state of apathy, you can discover the underlying programs by asking yourself what you're trying to prove. Are you trying to prove that life is rotten? That this is a hopeless world? That it wasn't your fault? That one can't find love? That happiness is impossible? What are you trying to justify? How much are you willing to pay to be "right"?

As you acknowledge and let go of the feelings that arise in response to these questions, the answers begin to appear. Write down what comes up for you as you do this.

_____

_____

_____

_____

_____

_____

_____

_____

_____

_____

_____

_____

_____

One of the biggest blocks to overcome in getting out of depression and apathy is that of blame. We have to be honest and realize that we are blaming because we choose to do so. This is true, no matter how justified the circumstances may appear to be.

Think of a circumstance where you may feel justified in blaming another person for what happened to you or for your feelings of unhappiness. Then list the payoffs you are getting in blaming instead of choosing to forgive in this particular situation by completing these sentences:

When I blame this person, I become . . .

_____

_____

_____

_____

_____

If I choose to forgive them, I now feel . . .

_____

_____

_____

_____

_____

_____

The psychological basis of all grief and mourning is attachment. Attachment and dependence occur because we feel incomplete within ourselves; therefore, we seek objects, people, relationships, places, and concepts to fulfill inner needs. Because they are unconsciously utilized to fulfill an inner need, they come to be identified as "mine." Loss of the object or person is experienced as a loss of our own self and an important part of our emotional economy.

To handle the fear of loss, we have to look at what purpose the person or object serves in our life. What emotional need is being fulfilled? What emotions would arise were we to lose them? Loss can be anticipated, and we can handle the various fears associated with the sense of loss by disassembling the emotional complexes that they represent, and letting go of the individual component feelings.

Let's say that you have a pet dog to which you have been attached for many years. It is obvious that Rover is getting older. You find that you don't like to think about his advanced age, feeling uncomfortable at the prospect of his death and putting it out of mind. As you catch yourself doing this, you realize that these feelings are warning signals and that you are not handling the emotional situation. And so, you ask yourself, "What purpose is Rover serving in my life? What is his emotional service to me?" In looking at this, some of the fear can be acknowledged and relinquished. Once the fear is let go, you don't have to resort to denial and pretend to yourself that Rover will live forever.

From the nature of the processes we have described, it becomes apparent that severe mourning, loss, and the pathological reactions that may ensue can be prevented by early recognition, and by preemptive surrender of the associated feelings while they are still mild and can be handled without excessive suffering.

Try this exercise in anticipating loss now with someone or something in your life that you're afraid of losing, and note the results here.

_____

_____

_____

_____

_____

_____

_____

_____

_____

_____

_____

_____

_____

_____

_____

_____

_____

Most of us carry a great deal of suppressed grief, which is due to the resistance to accepting that state and allowing the grief to expend itself. With the courage to face our inner feelings and let them go, we thus move on to the levels of acceptance and eventually peace.

If we don't resist the feeling of grief and totally surrender to it, it will run out in about 10–20 minutes; then it will stop for variable lengths of time. If we keep surrendering to it every time it comes up, then it will eventually run out. We just have to allow ourselves to experience it fully. If we resist the grief, then it will go on and on. When we let go of a lot of grief we've been holding for years, however, our friends and family will notice a change in our facial expression, our step will be lighter, and we will look younger.

Can you recall something in your life that you still feel some grief about—for example, a loss of a relationship, job, loved one, or pet? Write it down and allow yourself to feel it fully for around 10–20 minutes. Journal about your experience.

_____

_____

_____

_____

_____

_____

_____

_____

_____

Next, in the pages that follow, write down the name of something or someone in your life that you would be afraid to lose and ask yourself what internal needs they are satisfying. Answer these questions:

- *What feeling would come up if I were to lose them?*

- *How can my inner emotional life be balanced so as to decrease the extent, degree, and number of attachments on external objects and people?*

- *Why am I so empty within myself that I have to search for solutions in the form of attachment and dependency on others?*

- *Where am I looking to get love rather than to give it?*

_____

_____

_____

_____

_____

_____

_____

_____

_____

_____

> *The more loving we are, the less vulnerable we are to grief and loss, and the less we need to seek attachments.*

What one holds in mind
tends to manifest.

The many faces of fear are familiar to us all. We have felt free-floating anxiety and panic. We have been paralyzed and frozen by fear, with its accompanying palpitations and apprehension. Worries are chronic fears.

Any thought we consistently hold in mind and give energy to will tend to come into our life according to the very form in which our mind has held it. Thus, fear engenders fearful thoughts. The more we hold these thoughts in mind, the more likely the feared event will happen in our life, which again reinforces our fear.

In the world of consciousness, like goes to like, so that fear attracts fear just as its corollary is true that love attracts love. The more fear we hold, the more fearful situations we attract to our life. Each fear requires additional energy to create a protective device until, finally, all of our energy is drained into our extensive defensive measures. The willingness to look at a fear and work with it until we are free of it brings about immediate rewards.

Bring to mind a paralyzing fear or inhibition that you have. For example, *I am extremely afraid of public speaking.* Then write down the limiting beliefs and thoughts in regards to this fear: What happens within your body? What emotions go through you? Go on to describe a situation you were in where this fear paralyzed you psychologically and physically. How would your life become freer or more satisfying if you were free of this fear?

_____

_____

_____

_____

_____

_____

_____

_____

_____

_____

_____

_____

_____

_____

Next, start applying the surrender technique to this fear. You could begin by taking one or two limiting thoughts and beliefs and let them go. For instance, *I can't speak in front of people because my voice cracks. (I let go of this.)* Notice if anything changes, and record the results below.

_____

_____

_____

_____

_____

_____

_____

_____

_____

_____

_____

_____

_____

_____

_____

One particular form of fear is what we call guilt. Guilt is always associated with a feeling of wrongness and potential punishment, either real or in fantasy. If punishment is not forthcoming in the external world, it expresses itself as self-punishment on an emotional level. Guilt accompanies all of the negative emotions and thus, where there is fear, there is guilt.

The psychological programming in our society is so extensive that, for most people, even relaxing and enjoying a vacation is a problem. (Guilt says we "should" be doing something else.) There is disappointment when immediate relaxation does not occur. There is restlessness and the endless pursuit of "fun" activities to avoid the pain of facing our own inner self. Most busy executives begin to secretly look forward to getting back to work while they are on vacation. They may outwardly grumble about their heavy workload, but when they return to the accustomed routine, they feel normal again.

We know how easy it is to sell self-condemnation to a guilt-ridden person or fear of some disease to a fearful person. The idea, for instance, that "colds are catching" is a good example. The thought that "everybody's got a cold" will be subscribed to by a person who has sufficient guilt, fear, and naïveté regarding the laws of consciousness. Because of guilt, a person unconsciously feels that they "deserve" a cold. Thus, the body, which is controlled by the mind's belief, manifests the cold. The person who has let go of the underlying negative energies of guilt and fear does not have a fearful mind that believes, "A cold is going around; I'll probably get it like everybody else."

The way to change our bodies is to change our thoughts and feelings. We must let go of negative thoughts and belief systems and shed the stress of negative emotions that give them energy. We have to cancel the negative programming that comes from the world, as well as our own belief systems.

Answer these questions about how your mind punishes you when you feel guilty:

- *What do my thoughts and feelings tell me?*
- *How does my body feel?*
- *Can I see that guilt is destructive and harmful, rather than beneficial as I have been told?*

_____

_____

_____

_____

_____

_____

_____

_____

_____

_____

_____

_____

_____

_____

_____

We fear that the inner voyage of discovery will lead us to some dreadful, awful truth. This is one of the fearful programs that the world has set up to prevent us from finding out the real truth. There is one thing the world does not want us to find out, and that is the truth about ourselves. Why? Because then we will become free.

Every great teacher since the beginning of time has said to look *within* and find the truth, for the truth of what we really are will set us free. If what is to be found within ourselves were something to feel guilty about, something that is rotten, evil, and negative, then all the world's great teachers would not advise us to look there. On the contrary, they would tell us to avoid it at all costs.

We all derive great benefit from liberating ourselves out of a fearful inhibition into successful functioning, because that learning process automatically spills over into many other areas of our life. We become more capable, free, and happy, and with that, there is an inner peace of mind.

Yet we have the unconscious fantasy that fear is keeping us alive because it is associated with our whole set of survival mechanisms. We have the idea that, if we were to let go of fear, our main defense mechanism, we would become vulnerable in some way. In reality, the truth is just the opposite. Fear is what blinds us to the real dangers of life. In fact, fear itself is the greatest danger that the human body faces. Fear and guilt are what bring about disease and failure in every area of our lives.

If, in looking at ourselves, we see that we have allowed the experience of our own nature to become blocked off by extensive fears, then we can rediscover the love within us by utilizing the mechanism of surrender and, thus, letting go of the clouds of negativity. By rediscovering this inner love, we rediscover the true source of happiness.

We could also take the same protective actions out of love rather than out of fear. Can we not care for our bodies because we appreciate and value them, rather than out of fear of disease and dying? Can we not be of service to others in our life out of love, rather than out of fear of losing them? Can we not be polite and courteous to strangers because we care for our fellow human beings, rather than because we fear losing their good opinion of us? Can we not do a good job because we care about the quality of our performance and our fellow workers or the recipients of our services, rather than just the fear of losing our jobs or pursuing our own ambition? Can we not accomplish more by cooperation, rather than by fearful competition?

Try this exercise now by recontextualizing any fears you have in a positive way.

_____

_____

_____

_____

_____

_____

_____

_____

_____

_____

_____

_____

Fear is healed by love.

_____

_____

_____

_____

_____

_____

_____

_____

_____

_____

_____

_____

_____

_____

_____

_____

_____

Because of being totally surrendered, the impossible became possible, manifesting itself effortlessly and rapidly.

The second state of the levels of consciousness is "energetic," concerning emotions of desire, anger, and pride—with personal self-gain as the primary motivating factor. Now, desire itself may range from a mild wanting to an obsessive craving for something or someone. The underlying quality of this emotion is its drivenness. The essential point of freedom is whether we have chosen consciously to fulfill a certain want, or whether we are just being blindly run by unconscious programs and belief systems.

The way something comes into our life is because we have chosen it. It was the result of our intention, or we made a decision for it. It has come into our life *in spite of desire*. The desiring was actually the obstacle to its achievement or acquisition. This is because desire literally means, "I do not have." In other words, if we say that we desire something, we are saying that it isn't ours. When we say that it isn't ours, we put a psychic distance between ourselves and what we want. This distance becomes the obstacle that consumes energy.

The impossible becomes possible as soon as we are totally surrendered. This is because wanting blocks receiving it and results in a fear of not getting it. The energy of desire is, in essence, a denial that what we want is ours for the asking.

This is a different way of looking at achieving goals than the one we are used to. We are used to associating ambition and success with such virtues as self-sacrifice, keeping our nose to the grindstone, tightening our belt, buckling down, and all the grimness of hard work. When we look at this whole picture, it sounds arduous, doesn't it? Well, it is. It involves struggle, and the struggle results from the block we have put in our own way because of desire.

When we are in a higher state of consciousness in which we have acknowledged and let go of desire, we are in a freer state altogether, and what is chosen manifests in our life effortlessly. We surrender the emotion of desire and, instead, merely choose the goal, picture it lovingly, and allow it to happen because we see that it is already ours.

In a lower state of consciousness, the universe is seen as negative and denying, frustrating, and reluctant. It is like a bad, stingy parent. In a higher state of consciousness, our experience of the universe changes. It now becomes like a giving, loving, unconditionally approving parent who wants us to have everything we want, and it is ours for the asking. This is creating a different context. It is giving the universe a different meaning.

As we experience the letting go of desires, we begin to see that what we have chosen will come into our life almost magically, because what we hold in mind tends to manifest. All we need to have and to do will automatically fall into place.

Write down your personal goals with all their details here, even if they seem impossible to attain.

_____

_____

_____

_____

_____

_____

_____

_____

_____

_____

_____

_____

_____

_____

_____

_____

_____

_____

_____

_____

_____

_____

Let go of the desire for them one by one, now and whenever the desire comes into your awareness. Instead, choose the goal, picture it lovingly, and allow it to happen because you see that it is already yours.

At the lower levels of consciousness, it is what we *have* that counts. It is what we *have* that we value. It is what we *have* that gives us our self-image of worth and position in the world.

Once we have proven to ourselves that we can have, that our basic needs can be fulfilled, that we have the power to provide for our own needs and those of others who are dependent upon us, the mind begins to become more interested in what it is that we *do*. Then what we *do* in the world is the basis of our value and how others rate us. As we move up in lovingness, our doingness is less and less preoccupied with self-service and becomes more and more oriented to being of service to others. As our consciousness grows, we see that service, which is lovingly oriented toward others, automatically results in the fulfill-ment of our own needs. (This does not mean sacrifice. Service is not sacrifice.) Eventually, we become convinced that our own needs are automatically fulfilled by the universe, and our actions become almost automatically loving.

At that point, it is no longer what we do in the world but what we *are* that counts. We have proven to ourselves that we can have what we need, that we can do almost anything, given the willingness. And now what we *are*, within ourselves and to others, becomes most import-ant. People now seek our company, not because of what we have, not because of what we do and society's labels, but because of what we have *become*. Because of the quality of our presence, people just want to be around us and experience us.

The way to become that exciting person whom people want to know is very easy. We simply picture the kind of person we want to be and surrender all the negative feelings and blocks that prevent us from being that. What happens, then, is that all we need to have and to do will automatically fall into place. This is because, in contrast to having and doing, the level of being has the most power and energy. When it is given priority, it automatically integrates and organizes one's activities.

Take some time now to picture the kind of person you want to be. Then focus on surrendering all the negative feelings and blocks that prevent you from being that. When you're finished, write about what this exercise brought up for you in the pages that follow.

> *The most successful people in the world are those who hold in mind the highest good of all concerned, including themselves.*

Inside of us, but out of awareness, is the truth that "I already know everything I need to know."

Paradoxically, one resistance to surrendering is due to the effectiveness of the technique. What happens is that we keep letting go when life is not going too well and we are beset by unpleasant emotions. As we finally surrender our way out of it and all is well, then we stop letting go. This is a mistake because, as good as we may feel, there is usually more to it. Take advantage of the higher states and the momentum of letting go. Keep on going because it will get better and better all the time.

Letting go gains a certain momentum. It is easy to keep it going once it is started. The higher we feel, the easier it is to let go. That's a good time to reach down and let go of some things that we wouldn't want to tackle if we were in the dumps. There is always a feeling to be let up and surrendered. When we are feeling good, the emotions are merely subtler.

Sometimes you will feel stuck with a particular feeling. Simply surrender to the feeling of being stuck. Just let it be there and don't resist it. If it doesn't disappear, see if you can let go of the feeling in bits and pieces. Then be sure to come back to this page to remind yourself of what to do when that feeing of being stuck arises again.

We are all powerful beings who have become unconscious of our own power; we have denied and projected it onto others out of guilt and our own sense of smallness. To that end, here is an interesting example of the denial of inner power. A man who was desperate for a job and pretty frantic about it was instructed on how to apply the letting go technique to his job situation. Because he was of a religious nature, he was advised to forget about getting a job, turn it over to God, and surrender his desire in the matter while staying open to what might happen. A week later, he recounted: "Well, the day after I surrendered wanting a job, nothing happened. Then I got a call from my brother-in-law, and I am going to be joining his firm. If it weren't for him, I never would have gotten a job. It's a good thing I didn't wait for God!"

This is a good example of what the mind has a tendency to do. It was this man's own surrender, of course, that brought in the call from his brother-in-law. He so frantically desired the job that the desire was blocking the fulfillment of that goal. When he let go of wanting a job, it quickly appeared within 24 hours. But the propensity of the mind is to disown one's own power and project it elsewhere onto the world. This is why people in their own estimation think they are powerless. They have the power, but they have merely projected it onto external forces.

The majority of what happens in our lifetime is the result of some decision we have made somewhere in the past, either consciously or unconsciously. Because this is so, it is very simple to see our past decisions by looking at our life and tracking backwards.

Take a moment now to write about a particular time you surrendered and a desired outcome appeared.

_____

_____

_____

_____

It is common for people to repress their anger, aggression, and hostility; they view anger as unpleasant, undignified, and even as a moral failure or spiritual setback. They do not realize that repressed anger is nonetheless the energy of anger and, if not acknowledged and worked through, it will have deleterious consequences to their health and overall progress.

A helpful approach is to view the energy of anger positively and to use it to fire up your ambitions and actions in a useful way. Think of a relationship or situation either past or present that is causing you to feel angry and resentful. Write down how this energy of anger can be focused in a positive way, toward achieving a goal or project. For example, *The energy of anger spurred me to wash the kitchen floor, which I had been putting off doing.*

_____

_____

_____

_____

_____

_____

_____

_____

_____

_____

The mind would like us to think that there is such a thing as "justified anger." This takes the form of moralistic indignation, which is propped up by vanity and pride. We like to think how "right" we are in a situation and how "wrong" the other people are. The price we pay for chronic anger and resentment is sickness and premature death. Is this worth the small satisfaction of being right?

Summarize a situation where you feel "justified" in being angry. Complete this sentence: *In this situation I am "right" and the other person is "wrong" because . . .* Then write down the secret emotional payoffs you are getting and the emotional costs.

_____

_____

_____

_____

_____

_____

_____

_____

_____

_____

_____

_____

_____

Just like all the other negative feelings we have discussed so far, pride is devoid of love. The prideful feeling "I have the answers" blocks our growth and development. The humble person cannot be humiliated, for they are immune to vulnerability, having let go of pride. In its place, they have an inner security, self-esteem, courage, peacefulness, and joy.

Some of the things that people typically feel prideful about are lifestyle, vocation, neighborhood, clothes, type of car, ancestry, country, political and religious belief systems. Make a list of all the things that you feel prideful about and see if you can let go of them one by one by asking the following questions:

- *What is the purpose of feeling prideful of this?*
- *What is the payoff of my pride?*
- *Why do I seek this payoff?*
- *What kind of reactions from others am I hoping to elicit?*
- *For what does my pride about this thing compensate?*
- *What do I have to realize about my true nature in order to let pride go without a feeling of loss?*

_____

_____

_____

_____

_____

_____

_____

Because pride is sometimes seen as a motivator of achievement, what would be its higher-level substitute? One answer would be joy. What is wrong with joy as the reward for successful achievement rather than pride? Pride carries with it the desire for recognition from others and, consequently, there is a vulnerability to anger and disappointment if it is not forthcoming at some point. If we achieve a certain goal for the pleasure, enjoyment, love of accomplishment, and inner joy that it brings to us, we are invulnerable to the reaction of others.

Gratitude is also one of the antidotes of pride. If we happen to be born with a high IQ, we can be grateful for it rather than take pride in it. It's not an accomplishment; we were born with it. If we are grateful for what has been given us and for what has been fulfilled through our God-given talents and endeavors, then we are in a peaceful state of mind and invulnerable to pain.

When we let go of pride, help comes into our life to address the problems with which we are struggling. We can experiment and prove the truth of that principle by picking one area in which we are having difficulty and thoroughly surrendering all the pride involved. When we do that, some surprising things begin to happen. Letting go of pride unlocks the door to receiving that which is the most beneficial to us. Are you willing to let go of pride and feeling superior to others? Know that where pride is absent, attack from others is also absent. And when you are willing to let go of the pseudosecurity of pride, you experience the real security that comes with courage, self-acceptance, and joy.

_____

_____

_____

_____

_____

Letting go is very valuable in areas such as politics and religion, which are so historically prone to elicit argument that they are tactically bypassed in polite society. We will find that if we love our religion, whatever it might be, no one will attack us. If we are prideful, however, we will have to avoid the entire subject, because anger will quickly arise as a byproduct of the pride. When we truly value something, we lift it aloft out of the demeaning target range of argument.

That which we truly cherish and revere is protected by our own reverence. If we tell somebody that we do something because we get enjoyment out of it, there is really nothing much they can say about it, is there? If we infer that we do it because we are *right* in doing it, we will instantly see their hackles go up because they, also, have an opinion on what is right.

Our values are preferences. We hold them because we love them, enjoy them, and get pleasure from them. If we hold them in that context, we will be left in peace to enjoy them.

If we look at opinions, we will see that they are a dime a dozen. We become much less vulnerable if we put our thoughts, ideas, and beliefs, which are all opinions, into a different context. We can view them as ideas that we like or dislike. We can see that it is primarily our emotions that are giving them any value in the first place. If we don't take a prideful stance about our opinions, then we're at liberty to change them.

Take some time now to write down your most cherished opinions (such as those concerning religion, politics, dietary regimens, parenting views, and so on). Then, one by one, see if you can replace pride with just loving them because of their beauty, inspirational quality, or serviceability. Then you will no longer need the pride of being "right."

Once we have consciously contacted the truth of our real beingness—the nature of our inner self with all of its true innocence, greatness, and nobility of the human spirit—we no longer need pride.

The hallmark of courage
is the knowledge and feeling
"I can." It is a positive state
in which we feel assured,
skillful, adequate, capable,
alive, loving, and giving,
with an overall zest for life.

The third and highest level of consciousness is the peaceful state. This is based upon the feelings of courage, acceptance, and love.

On the level of courage, we really start becoming conscious. It dawns on us that we have the freedom and capacity to choose. We no longer have to be the victim, and freedom in the psychological, emotional, and spiritual sense is possible. We know that it is not necessary to endure the pain and suffering of the negative emotions or their interference with the satisfactions of life.

Now, when we are comfortable, there is a temptation to stop using the letting go technique and only resume it in emergency situations, or when negative feelings again become painful and necessitate our attention. However, there is more yet to be had. Because there is always a feeling going on which can be surrendered, the continuation of the process will lead to greater and greater benefits.

Continual surrender will bring about constant, subtle changes, especially when it comes to our capacity for love. The radiation of love is akin to the energy of the sunlight. As the dark clouds of negativity are removed, this energy, and our capacity to accept it and radiate it outward, increases progressively. Love empowers us, and the people around us, to do things that we would not be capable of otherwise.

We have to come up to the level of courage and look at our worst feelings and admit that they are part of the condition of being human, and remember that we are only held accountable for what we do with them. It is obvious that negative feelings take an enormous emotional toll on our own inner selves. That reason alone is sufficient to warrant looking at them and letting them go.

A common example is when someone is silently angry toward us. We sense that something is wrong even though nothing is said. Even if the person specifically says that nothing is wrong, we feel the energy of anger and upset.

Contemplate this, and then write down your own example of when you felt the energy of someone else's silent reaction toward you, but nothing was verbalized outwardly. Bring to mind the emotions and thoughts you felt in this situation:

- *Did I feel confused, helpless?*

- *Did I feel guilty, like I did something wrong?*

- *Did I feel angry?*

- *What did I want to do or not do?*

- *Did I want to "smooth things over" and make it better, or walk away and have nothing to do with the person?*

- *What is a positive step I could take in this situation?*

_____

_____

_____

_____

_____

With courage there is the willingness to take chances and let go of former securities. There is the willingness to grow and benefit from new experiences. This involves the capacity to admit mistakes without indulging in guilt and self-recrimination. Our sense of worth is not diminished by looking at areas that need improvement. We are able to admit there are problems without being diminished.

Write about an area of your life or a relationship or loss that you have avoided looking at previously but now have the courage to acknowledge, examine, and let go.

_____

_____

_____

_____

_____

_____

_____

_____

_____

_____

_____

_____

_____

_____

_____

_____

_____

_____

_____

_____

_____

_____

_____

_____

_____

_____

_____

When you're done, ask yourself if you can now see the freedom in not having to defend the mistake you think you made.

Love is a way of being that transforms everything around us because of the radiation of that energy. It happens on its own. We don't have to "do" anything, and we don't have to call it anything. Love is the energy that transfigures every situation. Love is the Ultimate Law of the Universe. It is the energy that radiates when the blocks to it have been surrendered. It is more than an emotion or a thought—it is a state of being. Love is what we have become through the pathway of surrender.

Once we become willing to give love, the discovery quickly follows that we are surrounded by love and merely didn't know how to access it. Love is actually present everywhere; its presence only needs to be realized.

During the day today, take mental note of the ways that love was present. Before you go to bed, write down the ways, no matter how large or small, in which love showed up for you.

_____

_____

_____

_____

_____

_____

_____

_____

_____

Love emanates from the heart. When we are in the presence of people who love each other, we pick up that energy. The love of our loved ones, pets, and friends is the love of Divinity for us. Each moment is possible only because of love. Being surrounded by the energy field of love brings gratitude. We are thankful for our life and for all the miracles of life.

Think about your life now, and contemplate all that you've been given. Write down what you are grateful for, regardless of how small or insignificant it seems.

_____

_____

_____

_____

_____

_____

_____

_____

_____

_____

_____

When you go to sleep tonight, be sure to give thanks that you were surrounded with love all day. Remember, each moment is possible only because of love.

Everyone is actually
doing the best they can with
what they have at the moment.
All of life is evolving toward
its perfection.

It is possible to forgive our own past, as well as that of others, and to heal past resentments. When we see the innocence in everyone, we can truly fulfill "loving our neighbor as ourselves."

It is also possible to see the hidden gift in past events about which we have been resentful—including their possible karmic significance. From the level of acceptance, it is possible to create a different context from which to view the past and thereby heal it.

Write about a past event or behavior that you haven't forgiven yourself for.

_____

_____

_____

_____

_____

_____

Can you see your innocence and that you were just doing the best you could with what your understanding was at the time? Can you apply this to others as well?

_____

_____

_____

_____

_____

In the state of acceptance, there is the feeling that nothing needs to be changed. This is different from resignation, where there are still residuals of the previous emotion left. There is reluctance and a delaying of the true recognition of the facts. Resignation says, "I don't like it, but I have to put up with it."

With acceptance, resistance to the true nature of the facts has been relinquished; thus, one of the signs of acceptance is serenity. With acceptance, the struggle is over and life begins anew. This consciousness level is one that we all long to achieve, for it enables us to find freedom from most of life's problems and to experience fulfillment and happiness. Here, the source of love is seen to be within ourselves, emanating from our own nature and reaching out to include others. Our lovingness radiates out naturally from the essence of our being, because many of the blocks to its awareness have been surrendered.

We discover that this lovingness is our nature, and it is what the great teachers mean by our true essence, our true Self. It is the aim of our Self to transcend the ego, that composite of all our negative feelings, programs, and thoughts, so that we are able to experience the inner essential nature.

In acceptance, we enjoy the experience of harmony and feel as though events are flowing. There is the feeling that nothing needs to be changed, everything is perfect and beautiful the way it is. We feel secure about the future and full of love and peace. We know that when the clouds are removed, the sun shines forth, and we discover that peace was the truth all along.

Stop and take a moment now to reflect upon this state. Sit quietly, breathe deeply, and feel the love and serenity within you. Remind yourself that everyone is actually doing the best they can with what they have at the moment, and all of life is evolving toward its perfection. Tune in to your Self and feel its presence. Know that it is always guiding you, if you'll only take the opportunity to listen.

Write about what you experienced on the pages that follow.

> *Surrender is the mechanism
> that uncovers the true nature
> of our existence.*

_____

_____

_____

_____

_____

_____

_____

_____

_____

_____

_____

_____

_____

_____

_____

_____

_____

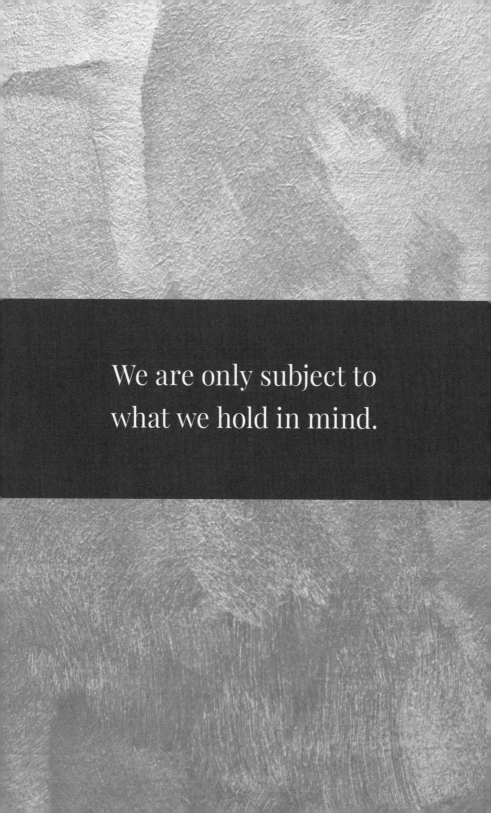

We are only subject to
what we hold in mind.

Letting go progressively reduces our personal "stress proneness," which correlates to the amount of suppressed and repressed feelings we have accumulated. Most people who learn and practice the technique lower their vulnerability to stress-related problems and illnesses, so they notice a progressive improvement in physical health and vitality.

Unfortunately, the inner experience of most people is marked by constant turmoil, most of which is psychological in origin. In other words, the main stress the majority of us have is not due to external stimuli, *but to the pressure of our own suppressed emotions.* These emotions become the primary stressor so that, even in a calm external environment, we are still subject to chronic, internal strife. *The more emotional pressure that is surrendered and let go, the less vulnerable we are to the stress response and stress-related diseases.*

It is we ourselves who create stressful reactions as a consequence of what we are holding within us. The suppressed feelings determine our belief systems and literally create events and incidents in the world, events that we, then, turn around and blame for our reactions.

Without a change of consciousness, there is no real reduction of stress. Only the consequences are ameliorated. Thought is powerful because it has a high rate of vibration. A thought is actually a thing; it has an energy pattern. The more energy we give it, the more power it has to manifest itself physically. The conscious use of the mechanism of surrender is most effective in addressing chronic stress-related illnesses. The way to change our bodies is to change our thoughts and feelings.

The body obeys the mind; therefore, the body tends to manifest what the mind believes, either consciously or unconsciously. The only power or energy that anything has over us is the power of belief that we give it.

Answer these questions:

- *What is my stress proneness?*
- *Am I feeling stressed right now?*
- *How are my external stress factors contributing to how I feel?*
- *What are the predominant internal feelings and thoughts that are contributing to the stressed state?*

Then, throughout the day, take deep breaths and surrender the feelings within that are contributing to the state of being stressed. Also, try to remind yourself that love stimulates endorphins and life energy, bringing a healing balm to stress-prone lives.

At the end of the day, review your experience. Did you notice any changes?

_____

_____

_____

_____

_____

_____

_____

_____

_____

_____

_____

_____

_____

_____

Our proneness to accept negative beliefs depends on how much negativity we are holding in the first place. A positive mind will refuse to accept negative thoughts and simply reject them as untrue for oneself.

To ascertain your own disease proneness, answer the following questions.

- *Do I worry about my health?*
- *Do I believe that the environment and foods are full of hidden dangers?*
- *Am I holding a lot of guilt and/or anger?*
- *Am I judgmental or holding resentments?*

_____

_____

_____

_____

_____

Then journal some specific issues for each one and practice letting them go.

_____

_____

_____

_____

_____

Next, make a list of the negative beliefs and fears you have about illness, disease, allergies, aging, and so on. Challenge the truth of them and practice surrendering on each one of them.

_____

_____

_____

_____

_____

_____

_____

_____

_____

_____

_____

_____

_____

_____

_____

It takes energy to hold down our feelings. As these feelings are relinquished, the energy that had been holding down the negativity is now freed for constructive uses. Consequent to letting go, there is an increase in available energy for creativity, growth, work, and interpersonal relationships. The most obvious and visible effect of letting go of negative feelings is a resumption of emotional and psychological growth and the solving of problems, which often are long-standing.

The effectiveness of the letting go mechanism in problem solving often is quite astonishing. Higher levels of functioning are seen to be automatic, easy to achieve, and available to everyone, often in a surprisingly short period of time.

Understanding the process involved here is very important, because it is quite different than the world's usual methods. The approach that brings fast and easy results is the following: *Don't look for answers; instead, let go of the feelings behind the question.* When we are surrendered on the feeling behind the question, we can let go of any other feelings that we might also have about what seems to be the problem. When we are finally and fully surrendered on all components, the answer will be there waiting for us. We won't have to look for it.

Consider how simple and easy this is as compared to the mind's usual long, drawn-out, inefficient attempts at problem-solving. Usually the mind hunts and pecks endlessly, fumbling around with first this possible answer and then that one. The reason the mind can't decide is because it is looking in the wrong place.

We feel pleasure and fulfillment as we begin to experience the powerful effects of eliminating the blocks to achievement and satisfaction in life.

Let's try it now. Begin by describing an interest or activity you have where you feel "ill at ease" and lack confidence in achieving success in this area, even though you want to. For example, *I would like to write a book, but . . .*

Next, answer these questions:

- *What are the blocks that are holding me back from doing it?*
- *What emotions are keeping me from trying it?*
- *What beliefs do I have that keep me from expressing myself through this interest or activity?*
- *What negative self-talk am I experiencing surrounding this?*

_____

_____

_____

_____

_____

_____

_____

_____

_____

_____

_____

_____

_____

_____

_____

After reviewing what you've written, take some time in the next couple of days and use the letting go method to work on surrendering these blocks. Come back and update this entry as needed.

_____

_____

_____

_____

_____

_____

_____

_____

_____

_____

_____

_____

_____

_____

One surprising observation about the mechanism of letting go is that major changes can take place very rapidly. Lifetime patterns can suddenly disappear, and long-standing inhibitions can be let go of in a matter of minutes, hours, or days. Rapid changes are accompanied by an increased aliveness. The life energy set free by the letting go of negativity now flows into positive attitudes, thoughts, and feelings, with a progressive increase of personal power.

When the negative blocks and "I can'ts" are removed, whole new areas of life open up to us. Success stems from doing what we like to do best, but most people are tied down to what they imagine they have to do. As limitations are relinquished, whole new avenues of creativity and expression become available. It is very common for people who use the letting go technique to suddenly come into abundance.

Take, for example, the young woman with a lot of natural musical talent who was spending most of her time at a boring job, which she felt she had to stick with for financial reasons. What she really liked to do was play musical instruments when she was alone at home. Because of a lack of self-confidence, she seldom played for other people, even close friends. After she began to let go of her inner limitations, her abilities and confidence grew so rapidly that she began to play in front of public gatherings. Her talent was well received, and a busy musical career ensued. She made a professional recording that was sufficiently successful that she could cut back to working part-time, and she began to pour more time and energy into a career that brought her great joy and satisfaction. Although she had known nothing about business, she started her own musical business and was soon distributing recordings in the U.S. and Europe. To her delight, she found that she was very successful by doing what she liked to do best. Her increasing vitality and happiness were apparent to everyone, and success spread to other areas of her life.

As we let go of the negative, we come into our own power. It happens of its own. Happiness was in there all along and now it shines forth after the blocks to it have been surrendered. We are now influencing everyone with whom we come in contact in a favorable way.

In the pages that follow, name an area of expression, no matter how seemingly small or insignificant, that has become a reality for you as a result of the letting go method. Write down the positive feelings you have about this newfound expression. Then congratulate yourself on the work you have done!

With the removal of negativity,
dynamic forces are unloosed, so
that what were once impossible dreams
now become actualized goals.

The goal of letting go is the
elimination of the very source
of all suffering and pain.

The replacement of a negative feeling by a higher one accounts for the many miracles we can experience in the course of life. These become more frequent as we continue to let go. As we surrender, life becomes more and more effortless. There is a constant increase in happiness and pleasure, which requires less and less from the outer world to be experienced. There is a diminution of needs and expectations of others. We stop looking "out there" for what we now experience as coming from within ourselves. We let go of the illusion that others are the source of our happiness. Instead of looking to get from others, we now look to give. Others now seek to be with us, instead of avoiding us.

Ultimately, all negative feelings stem from the same source. When enough negative feelings have been relinquished, that source reveals itself. When that source itself is let go of and disidentified with, the ego dissolves. The source of suffering, therefore, loses the very basis of its power.

Each of us has a limit to the number of negative feelings we have stored up. When the pressure behind an emotion has been let go, that emotion no longer occurs. For instance, if fear is constantly surrendered for a period of time, eventually it runs out. It then becomes difficult or almost impossible to feel further fear. It takes progressively more and more of a stimulus to elicit it, until the person who has surrendered so much fear actually has to search for it diligently. The energy of fear simply isn't there anymore. Anger also progressively diminishes so that even a major provocation fails to elicit it. A person with little fear or anger feels primarily love all of the time and experiences a loving acceptance of events, people, and the vicissitudes of life.

The goal of surrender is transcendence.

Now, let's look at the effect that the mechanism of surrender has on those areas of life with which most people are concerned, beginning with health.

The average person is preoccupied with the body, its functioning, performance, appearance, and survival. The average mind is beleaguered with worries, fears of sickness, suffering, disease, and death; therefore, the mind sets about defending the body in a great variety of ways. Underlying all of this concern is the unconscious equation, "I am a body." Be aware of how much energy is drained by this constant preoccupation with the body.

It becomes progressively obvious that the body is not experiencing itself at all. On the contrary, it is the mind that is experiencing the body. Without the mind, the body cannot be perceived at all. The arm cannot experience its armness. Only the mind can experience the armness. This, of course, is the very basis of anesthesia. When the mind is asleep, the body has no sensation. It slowly dawns on us that, in fact, the body doesn't have any sensation; only the mind is capable of that function.

This is a very important shift of consciousness because now the preoccupation is not with the body and defending it. The focus of attention now shifts to the mind, which is where the greater power lies. As we shift our thoughts, feelings, and perceptions, we begin to notice that the body follows suit.

As we begin letting go of all these fears, canceling the belief systems and reaffirming that our true Self is Infinite and not subject to limitations, we move into a higher state of health, wellness, and vital energy. In the state of total surrender, the body is barely perceived at all, and we shift our perception from "I *am* a body" to "I *have* a body."

A helpful exercise is to start using the phrase, "I am an Infinite Being, not subject to _____." Put into the blank space whatever disease or substance that the mind has been programmed to see as a possible "danger" for you. Try this now with whatever has previously concerned you with your health.

To the mind that holds limiting belief systems and negative thoughts and feelings, money is a "problem," bringing us a feeling of financial limitation, lack, and deprivation.

The unconscious brings to us what it thinks we deserve. If our view of ourselves is small, limited, and miserly, then the unconscious will bring those economic conditions into our life. Attitudes about money can be discovered when you look at the many things that it means, so it can be very useful to sit down and consciously delineate this.

As we do this exercise, we have the surprising discovery that money in and of itself is not the most basic issue. More important than money itself are the emotional gratifications that we hope will be ours with the use of that money.

Let's say that, behind the desire for money, we discover that one of our goals is to be respected and valued. We have found out that it isn't money itself that we are interested in; rather, it is our self-respect and a feeling of inner worth. We see that money was just a tool to achieve something else and that, as a matter of fact, it isn't money that we want at all but the self-respect and esteem we thought it would bring us.

It will also dawn on us that the goals we thought money would bring us *can be achieved directly.* The higher our inner self-esteem, the less we need the approval of others. As we uncover these awarenesses, money takes on a different meaning in each area of life. Money now becomes subservient to higher goals rather than an end unto itself.

Without being conscious of what money means to us emotionally, we allow ourselves to be run by our unconscious beliefs about it. It is like the millionaire who keeps piling up more and more millions, but there never seems to be enough. Why is that? It is because he has never stopped to look at what money really means to him. If we obsessively chase after money or other symbols of wealth, it is because our inner self-worth is so small that it takes a huge amount of money to compensate for it. The inner insecurity is so extensive that no amount of money can overcome it.

Examine your feelings about this subject on the following pages. Under the heading "Money," write down what its real meanings are to you in all the various avenues of life, and then describe the feelings that are associated with each area. When you've finished, begin to surrender each negative feeling and attitude.

When we are in the surrendered state, we are free from that inner smallness, insecurity, and low self-esteem; then money becomes merely a tool to achieve our goals in the world.

_____

_____

_____

_____

_____

_____

_____

_____

_____

_____

_____

_____

_____

As negative thoughts, feelings, and attitudes are relinquished, we re-own the power that we had given over to the world.

Much of the attraction of the world is due to the glamorization that we have projected onto it. Ask yourself the following:

- *Is it really all that money that I want, or is it the glamour that I have attached to it?*

- *What is it that I want from that job title or from that designation of "Dr.," "Esq.," or "Rev."?*

- *Do I desire the responsibility and activities that go along with that job title or designation, or the glamour and esteem associated with it?*

- *Do I really love that person, or am I in love with the glamour I have projected onto them?*

_____

_____

_____

_____

The more we let go, the more we deglamorize the world. The more it is deglamorized, the less it runs us. We are not at the effect of glamour and can no longer be manipulated by it. We are no longer vulnerable to the professional programmers of the media and the political and social arenas. We are no longer at the effect of an inner need for approval from others.

We begin to love people for what they are, not for what they can do for us. We no longer need to exploit others or try to win them over. As our own level of guilt decreases, our self-esteem expands. Because relationships are based on honesty, and they exist and function on a higher plane, there is no longer a fear of alienation or feeling of aloneness. The surrendered person no longer needs others for personal fulfillment but is with them out of choice because of love and enjoyment. Compassion for others and for their humanness transforms life and all relationships.

The way to facilitate satisfaction in relationships is to lovingly picture the best possible outcome. Make sure it is mutually beneficial: a win-win situation. Let go of all the negative feelings and merely hold the picture in mind. If we have negative feelings, it is best to remember that they are not our real inner Self. They are learned programs we have inherited from being human. Nobody is exempt from them; everyone from the highest to the lowest has an ego. Even the few who are enlightened had an ego at one time before it was finally transcended. This is the human condition. To be able to *observe our feelings honestly requires a nonjudgmental attitude.*

We can tell if we are really surrendered when we feel okay either way; it's okay with us if it happens, and it's okay with us if it doesn't. Therefore, to be surrendered does not mean to be passive. It is being active in a positive way.

When we are surrendered, there is no longer the pressure of time. Frustration comes from wanting a thing now instead of letting it happen naturally in its own time. Patience is an automatic side effect of letting go, and we know how easy it is to get along with patient people. Notice that patient people usually get what they want in the end.

Write down what your experience with this has been.

_____

_____

_____

_____

_____

_____

Happiness can be experienced directly, independent of health or wealth. However, as a result of negative feelings, thoughts, and attitudes, together with the constant judgment and criticism of other people, we often feel separated from others. Because of this feeling of inner aloneness and separation, relationships take on the form of attachments, with all the fear, anger, and jealousy that accompany any threat to those attachments. This makes us feel weak and limited. We also project our inner thoughts and feelings onto the world, making it look like a fearful place and literally bringing into our life experience fearful events because these fears are held in mind.

Because of this inner chaos, the average person must of necessity stay unconscious at all times through television, radio, emails, texting, podcasts, websites, projects, work, phone calls, reading, appointments, errands, social engagements, drugs, alcohol, and so forth to get the mind off the self and its mental chatter. We tend to do just about anything to avoid facing that feeling of inner emptiness. Understand that there is nothing wrong with any of these activities in and of themselves. In a state of inner freedom, these same events and experiences take on a totally different significance—the identical activities can stem from an inner sense of happiness, self-worth, and completeness.

Write down all the things you do in a day to stay unconscious. For example, *I watch TV to avoid responsibility or to zone out* or *I listen to music to tune out the chatter in my mind.* Then examine the states of consciousness in doing these activities, the state of awareness, and the manner in which these activities are perceived, pursued, and experienced.

Another law of consciousness is: *Our feelings and thoughts always have an effect on other people and affect our relationships, whether these thoughts or feelings are verbalized, expressed, or not.* We can likely intuit the truth of this from our own experience. We generally know, for example, when someone is angry toward us, even if they say nothing about it. Sensing their feelings, we might ask, "Is something wrong?" Even when they reply, "Oh nothing," we are still aware of the energy of anger and upset.

Most everyone is brought up to believe that our thoughts and feelings are private affairs and nobody else's business, that all minds are separated, and that emotions happen only within the confines of the body. As we begin to investigate this area, we find that often the set of feelings we hold about another person is mirrored back to us by their attitude and that, when we change our inner attitude about them, their attitude changes abruptly. We are unconsciously influencing others all the time because of the feelings we hold about them.

With observation, it is quite clear that negative feelings reverberate and boomerang back to us, and profoundly affect our relationships. The other person merely mirrors back what we are projecting onto them. When the inner feelings are relinquished, the way in which we see the situation changes, and we are often surprised by the abruptness with which feelings of forgiveness suddenly arise and the relationship becomes transformed, even though on the external level we did or said nothing to express this inner change.

Try this exercise now, by bringing to mind a person in your life that you have an unkind attitude toward. Write down the negative feelings you have toward this person. Since this is your journal, honestly express everything you feel in this moment about this person and why.

_____

_____

_____

_____

When you feel that all the negative feelings have been written down and released, at least on paper, look within yourself and see if you sense any higher feelings, perhaps *calm, peace, forgiveness, a sense of being okay,* or *acceptance.*

_____

_____

_____

Come back here and note if anything changes in your relationship with this person, now that you have let go of your negative feelings toward them.

_____

_____

_____

_____

_____

_____

_____

_____

_____

_____

_____

We first have to be aware of what is really going on inside of us before we can do anything about it. As we let go of a feeling, it is replaced by a higher one. The only purpose for recognizing and admitting a feeling is so that we can relinquish it. To be surrendered means that we are willing to relinquish a feeling by allowing ourselves just to experience it and not to change it. Resistance is what keeps it there in the first place. So if we have difficulty in relinquishing a feeling, it helps merely to look at the intent of that feeling.

Write down the feeling you are having difficulty with releasing in the form of a statement. For example, *I am feeling resentful toward Mary for treating me unfairly.*

_____

_____

_____

_____

_____

_____

_____

_____

_____

_____

_____

Then answer these questions:

- *What is the purpose of it?*
- *What is the supposed purposeful effect on the other person?*
- *What is their likely response?*
- *Do I actually want that?*

Next, think about this: If this were the last day of your life, would that really be what you wanted? Well, this *is* the last day of your life—your old life with all its conflicts, anxiety, and fear. That is the price you have paid for holding on to the old.

As you relinquish the negative suppressed feelings from all the programs you have internalized, they are automatically replaced by the higher ones. You'll become happier and lighter and so will the people around you.

Moving on to the topic of careers, our thoughts determine the extent to which we manifest our talents and abilities, and they set the quality and quantity of our successes and failures. But it is our feelings that determine and produce the kind of thinking that will lead us to success or failure in any endeavor. Feelings are the key to the expansion or constriction of our talents, abilities, and actions.

Negative feelings are always unpleasant and range from mildly uncomfortable to painful. Suppressing these feelings does not make them disappear, but instead they will reemerge as negative thoughts. Negativity does not exist within a situation or event; rather, it resides in our reaction to the situation as we see it. When negative feelings are acknowledged and relinquished, the situation can rapidly change in appearance from impossible to easily manageable, workable, and even quite useful. Once our feelings are recognized, it becomes obvious that they work against us. They drain our efforts and impede our success in the world.

Review your work situation and write about any negative feelings like anger, grief, anxiety, envy, self-doubt, desire for approval, lack, et cetera, that you may be currently experiencing.

_____

_____

_____

_____

_____

_____

_____

_____

_____

_____

_____

_____

_____

_____

_____

In the workplace, many people think they should suppress their feelings of resentment; however, this approach does not handle the problem and the tensions will fester. With the letting go technique, go within yourself and acknowledge the negative feelings as they arise. Let them come up without suppressing them and without venting them. And then shift your attention from the feelings to something else. Let the feelings be there and let them go.

Often, surrendering to what appears to be an impossible situation quickly turns into a positive experience. This is exemplified by the case of someone who had been working in an art gallery. Things were slow; she hadn't made a sale in weeks. She tried a number of consciousness techniques with herself and worked very hard at it, but nothing came of it. Her frustration mounted progressively, with the accompanying feeling of "I can't."

Finally, in desperation, she just let go completely and surrendered all of her pent-up feelings. Inside of herself, she suddenly felt free of all the efforting, trying, and striving. The inner tension disappeared and, instead, she felt at peace as she went to work that morning at the gallery. Within the first hour at work, she sold two copies of a sculpture (which, interestingly enough, was titled _Letting Go_).

Keep in mind that positive feelings like joy, happiness, and security will flow naturally when negative feelings are not in action. Nothing needs to be done to acquire positive feelings, as they are part and parcel of our natural state. This positive inner state is always there, and it is merely covered over by suppressed negative feelings. The freeing up of abilities, creative ideas, talents, and resourcefulness occurs automatically as a result of the positive state of mind that ensues when the negative aspects have been surrendered.

Write down some of the positive feelings you have toward your work. Can you see how these feelings contribute to your productiveness and capabilities?

_____

_____

_____

_____

_____

_____

_____

_____

_____

_____

_____

_____

As you apply the letting go technique to every area of life, without exception, the energy of spiritual work gets stronger and stronger. There is a fixity of attention, the relentless staying with a method, no matter what is going on.

Serious spiritual work is a continuous willingness to let things go as they arise. It is the willingness to surrender wanting to control everything as it arises, the willingness to surrender wanting to change it, and to have it our way. Very often there will be illusions about the nature of Reality that also have to be let go. That there's a "good" and a "bad," a desirable and a non-desirable, is all in the mind. In Reality, the sun shines and then the clouds come; the rain falls and the grass grows up and dies; the stock market goes up and down; age comes and goes; people arrive and leave. And so there's the ebb and flow. If you are at this one point of the cycle, there's no use crying about it because it will cycle itself out. By surrendering to whatever is cycling up, it eventually disappears. You disappear it by choosing to be one with it and refusing to want to change it as it arises. Do this continuously no matter what, nonstop.

Eventually, everything is surrendered that stands in the way of the Presence. The Presence is so obvious, so startling, so overwhelming, that there's no question about it. It is profound, total, all-encompassing, absolutely overwhelming, totally transforming, and completely unmistakable. When everything is surrendered that stands in the way, "It" is there, shining brilliantly forth.

Instead of viewing this as something in the future, *own it now*. The reason you're not experiencing this state of total peace and timelessness is because it is being resisted. It is being resisted because you are trying to control the moment. If you let go of trying to control your experience of the moment, and if you constantly surrender it like a tone of music, then you live on the crest of this exact alwaysness.

On the pages that follow, write about the progress you've made. Continue to do this periodically, so you have a concrete reminder of how far you have come.

The energy field of creative genius is available and waiting for us as soon as we surrender the clouds of negativity that prevent its revelation to us.

Enlightenment is not something that occurs in the future, after 50 years of sitting cross-legged and saying "OM." It is right here, in this instant.

As we wrap up here, know that the secret to using this mechanism more often and more consistently is, first of all, the wish to do so. That is Step #1. You have to want to be free of the feeling more than you want to keep it. Sometimes it is just a matter of remembering, and you can use some kind of a cue card to remind you. Here are some other ideas:

1. Establish a routine. It is very good to start the day by surrendering your thoughts and feelings about your expectations, to picture the way you would like the day to go, and to let go of all negative thoughts that would interfere with the day going in that way. Then, at the end of the day, sit down and surrender anything that came up during the course of the day that you overlooked or didn't have time to pay attention to. This is called "cleaning up," and most people find that they sleep better.

2. Supplement this journal with a notebook in which you write down your successes. You might put down the goal of constant surrendering and follow it up with what the results were.

3. Let go of your resistance to surrendering and, as you start the day, reaffirm your intention to let go of all negativity that day. You can also reaffirm that you are free not to surrender. After all, it is totally a matter of choice. Let go of any feeling of compulsion about it. There isn't any "should."

Remember, we think that somehow, if we hang on to that feeling, it is going to get us what we want. If we get stuck in a feeling, it is useful to look at the question of what we think we have accomplished by hanging on to it. We will almost always find that we have a fantasy that it will have some effect on some other person and change their behavior or attitudes toward us. If we let go of that, we become willing to let go of the feeling.

Let all of these resistances come up, accept them, and let them go. Clarify your intention to become a happier, more loving and peaceful person, and you will be on your way to enlightenment, where you have removed your inner blocks once and for all.

Journal Review

Finally, here is a list of some of the truths explained in this *Letting Go Guided Journal*. Read the list and select the ones that really speak to you. Journal what you have already discovered for yourself about them and also write down what you would like to understand at an even deeper level.

- *We surrender a feeling by allowing it to be there without condemning, judging, or resisting it. We simply look at it, observe it, and allow it to be felt without trying to modify it. With the willingness to relinquish a feeling, it will run out in due time.*

- *Thoughts are caused by suppressed and repressed feelings. When a feeling is let go, thousands or even millions of thoughts that were activated by that feeling disappear.*

- *A strong feeling may recur, which means there is more of it to be recognized and surrendered.*

- *In order to relinquish a feeling, sometimes it is necessary to acknowledge and let go of the underlying payoff of it (e.g., the "thrill" of anger and the "juice" of sympathy from being a helpless victim).*

- *Feelings are not the real self. Whereas feelings are programs that come and go, the real inner Self always stays the same; therefore, it is necessary to stop identifying transient feelings as yourself.*

- No matter what is going on in life, keep the steadfast intention to surrender negative feelings as they arise.

- Make a decision that freedom is more desirable than a negative feeling.

- Choose to surrender negative feelings rather than express them.

- Notice that letting go is accompanied by a subtle, overall lighter feeling within yourself.

- Relinquish negative feelings but share positive ones.

- Relinquishing a desire does not mean that you won't get what you want. It merely clears the way for it to happen.

- "Like goes to like." Associate with people who are using the same or similar motivation and who have the intention to expand their consciousness and to heal.

- Be aware that your inner state is known and transmitted. The people around you will intuit what you are feeling and thinking, even if you don't verbalize it.

- Persistence pays off. Some symptoms or illnesses may disappear promptly; others may take months or years if the condition is very chronic.

- Let go of resisting the technique. Start the day with it. At the end of the day, take time out to relinquish any negative feelings left over from the day's activities.

- You are only subject to what you hold in mind. You are only subject to a negative thought or belief if you consciously or unconsciously say that it applies to you.

- Instead of putting labels and names on feelings, we can simply feel the feelings and let go of the energy behind them. It is not necessary to label a feeling "fear" in order to be aware of its energy and relinquish that energy.

The Map of Consciousness®

God-view	Life-view	Level		Log	Emotion	Process
Self	Is	Enlightenment	⇧	700-1000	Ineffable	Pure Consciousness
All-Being	Perfect	Peace	⇧	600	Bliss	Illumination
One	Complete	Joy	⇧	540	Serenity	Transfiguration
Loving	Benign	Love	⇧	500	Reverence	Revelation
Wise	Meaningful	Reason	⇧	400	Understanding	Abstraction
Merciful	Harmonious	Acceptance	⇧	350	Forgiveness	Transcendence
Inspiring	Hopeful	Willingness	⇧	310	Optimism	Intention
Enabling	Satisfactory	Neutrality	⇧	250	Trust	Release
Permitting	Feasible	Courage	⇕	200	Affirmation	Empowerment
Indifferent	Demanding	Pride	⇩	175	Scorn	Inflation
Vengeful	Antagonistic	Anger	⇩	150	Hate	Aggression
Denying	Disappointing	Desire	⇩	125	Craving	Enslavement
Punitive	Frightening	Fear	⇩	100	Anxiety	Withdrawal
Disdainful	Tragic	Grief	⇩	75	Regret	Despondency
Condemning	Hopeless	Apathy	⇩	50	Despair	Abdication
Vindictive	Evil	Guilt	⇩	30	Blame	Destruction
Despising	Miserable	Shame	⇩	20	Humiliation	Elimination

About the Author

David R. Hawkins, M.D., Ph.D. (1927–2012), was director of the Institute for Spiritual Research, Inc., and founder of the Path of Devotional Nonduality. He was renowned as a pioneering researcher in the field of consciousness as well as an author, lecturer, clinician, physician, and scientist. He served as an advisor to Catholic and Protestant churches, and Buddhist monasteries; appeared on major network television and radio programs; and lectured widely at such places as Westminster Abbey, the Oxford Forum, the University of Notre Dame, and Harvard University. His life was devoted to the upliftment of mankind until his death in 2012.

For more information on Dr. Hawkins's work, visit veritaspub.com.

Also by
David R. Hawkins, M.D., Ph.D.

Books

Book of Slides: The Complete Collection Presented
at the 2002–2011 Lectures with Clarifications

Daily Reflections from Dr. David R. Hawkins:
365 Contemplations on Surrender, Healing, and Consciousness

Discovery of the Presence of God: Devotional Nonduality

The Ego Is Not the Real You: Wisdom to
Transcend the Mind and Realize the Self

The Eye of the I: From Which Nothing Is Hidden

Healing and Recovery

I: Reality and Subjectivity

Letting Go: The Pathway of Surrender

The Map of Consciousness Explained: A Proven Energy
Scale to Actualize Your Ultimate Potential

Power vs. Force: The Hidden Determinants of Human Behavior

Reality, Spirituality, and Modern Man

Success Is for You: Using Heart-Centered Principles
for Lasting Abundance and Fulfillment

Transcending the Levels of Consciousness:
The Stairway to Enlightenment

Truth vs. Falsehood: How to Tell the Difference

The Wisdom of Dr. David R. Hawkins: Classic Teachings on Spiritual Truth and Enlightenment

Audio Programs

How to Surrender to God

Live Life as a Prayer

The Map of Consciousness Explained

Please visit:

Hay House USA: www.hayhouse.com®
Hay House Australia: www.hayhouse.com.au
Hay House UK: www.hayhouse.co.uk
Hay House India: www.hayhouse.co.in

Hay House Titles
of Related Interest

YOU CAN HEAL YOUR LIFE, the movie, starring
Louise Hay & Friends
(available as an online streaming video)
www.hayhouse.com/louise-movie

THE SHIFT, the movie,
starring Dr. Wayne W. Dyer
(available as an online streaming video)
www.hayhouse.com/the-shift-movie

THE COSMIC JOURNAL, by Yanik Silver

*THE GIFT OF GRATITUDE: A Guided Journal
for Counting Your Blessings,* by Louise Hay

*LIVING YOUR PURPOSE JOURNAL: A Guided Path
to Finding Success and Inner Peace,* by Dr. Wayne W. Dyer

SUPER ATTRACTOR JOURNAL, by Gabrielle Bernstein

THE UNIVERSE HAS YOUR BACK JOURNAL,
by Gabrielle Bernstein

All of the above are available at your local bookstore,
or may be ordered by contacting Hay House (see next page).